Words around us

A picture word book

ISBN 0-88625-124-9

© 1986 Hayes Publishing Ltd.
Burlington, Ontario

3312 Mainway, Burlington, Ontario L7M 1A7, Canada
2045 Niagara Falls Blvd., Unit 14, Niagara Falls, NY 14304, U.S.A.

For Jesse

Words around us

A picture word book

Tim O'Halloran

AROUND THE HOUSE

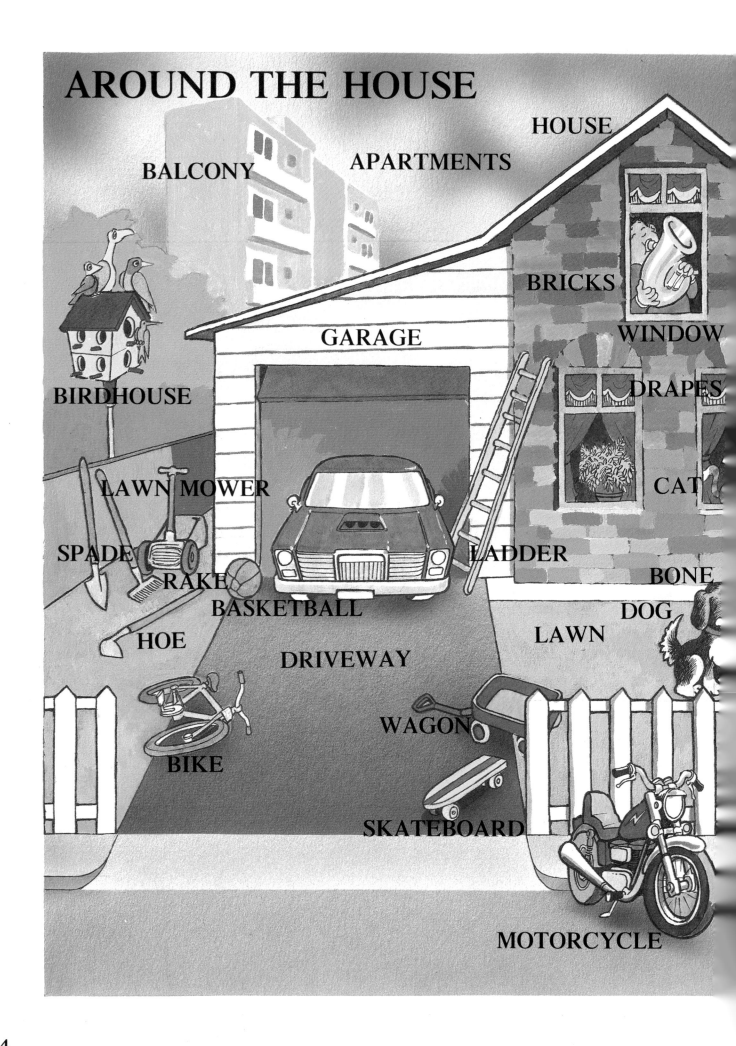

BALCONY

APARTMENTS

HOUSE

BRICKS

WINDOW

BIRDHOUSE

GARAGE

DRAPES

LAWN MOWER

CAT

SPADE

LADDER

BONE

RAKE

BASKETBALL

DOG

HOE

LAWN

DRIVEWAY

BIKE

WAGON

SKATEBOARD

MOTORCYCLE

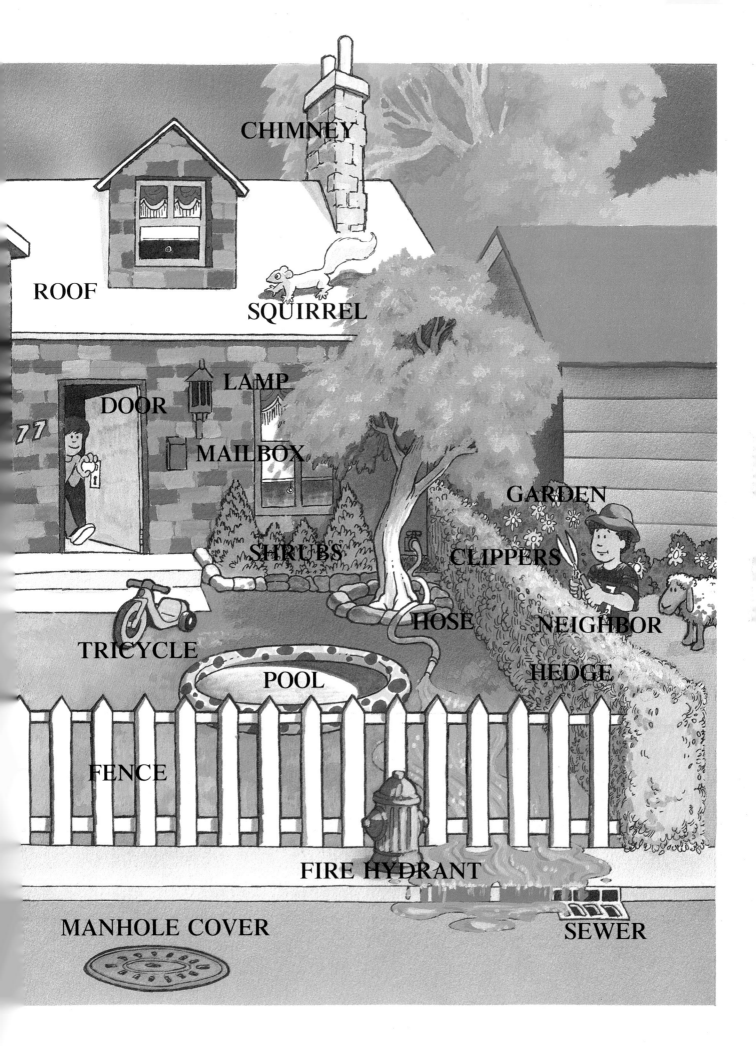

CHIMNEY

ROOF

SQUIRREL

LAMP

DOOR

MAILBOX

GARDEN

SHRUBS

CLIPPERS

NEIGHBOR

HOSE

TRICYCLE

HEDGE

POOL

FENCE

FIRE HYDRANT

MANHOLE COVER

SEWER

77

RISE AND SHINE

DRESSER

ALARM CLOCK

HEADBOARD

YAWN

PILLOW

LAMP

DRAWER

MATTRESS

BED

BLANKET   BEDSPREAD

SHEET

TOY BOX

Each picture spread in this book contains
something that does not belong. Can you find and
name it?

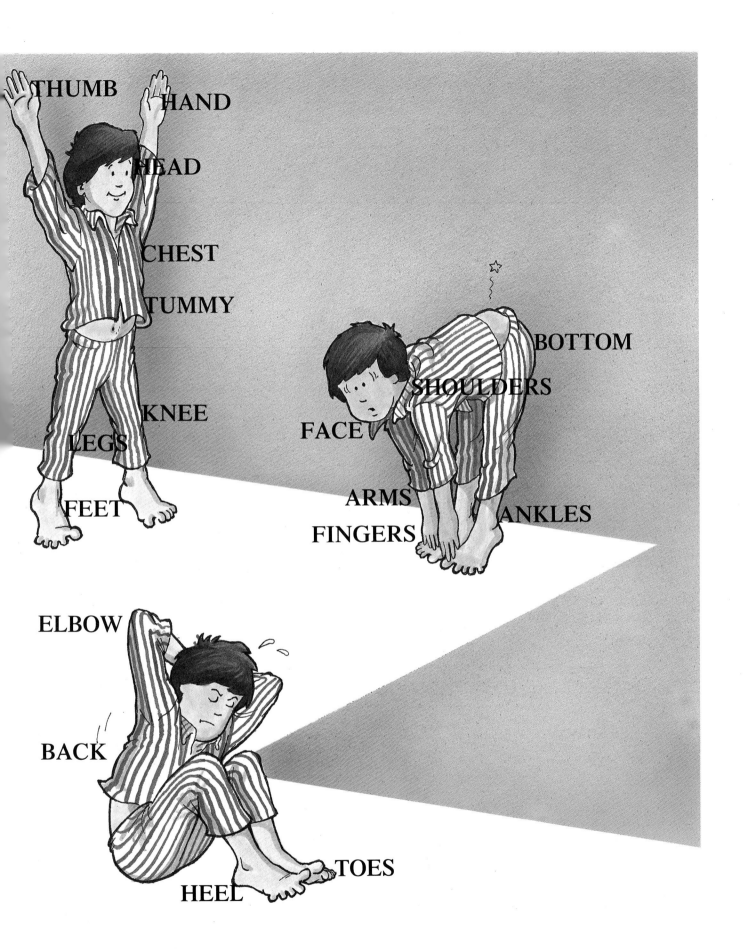

THUMB

HAND

HEAD

CHEST

TUMMY

KNEE

LEGS

FEET

BOTTOM

SHOULDERS

FACE

ARMS

FINGERS

ANKLES

ELBOW

BACK

TOES

HEEL

WASHING UP

HAIR DRYER

LIGHT

MIRROR

HAIR

EYES

TOOTHBRUSH

EARS

NOSE

TOOTHPASTE

TEETH

SPONGE

NECK

BRUSH

TAP

BATHROBE

SOAP

SINK

SHOWER

BUBBLES

TISSUE

BATHTUB

TOILET

BATH MAT

FACE CLOTH

SHAVING CREAM

SHAMPOO

TOWEL

COTTON BALLS

RAZOR

COMB

SHELF

9

GETTING DRESSED

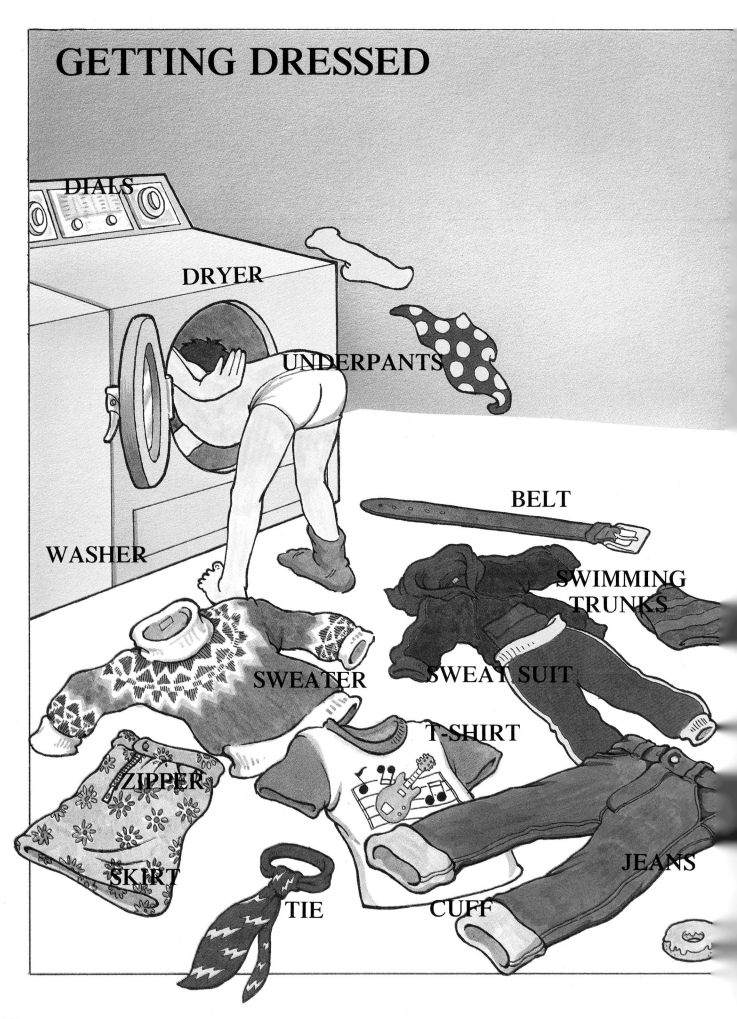

DIALS

DRYER

UNDERPANTS

BELT

SWIMMING
TRUNKS

WASHER

SWEATER

SWEAT SUIT

T-SHIRT

ZIPPER

SKIRT

TIE

CUFF

JEANS

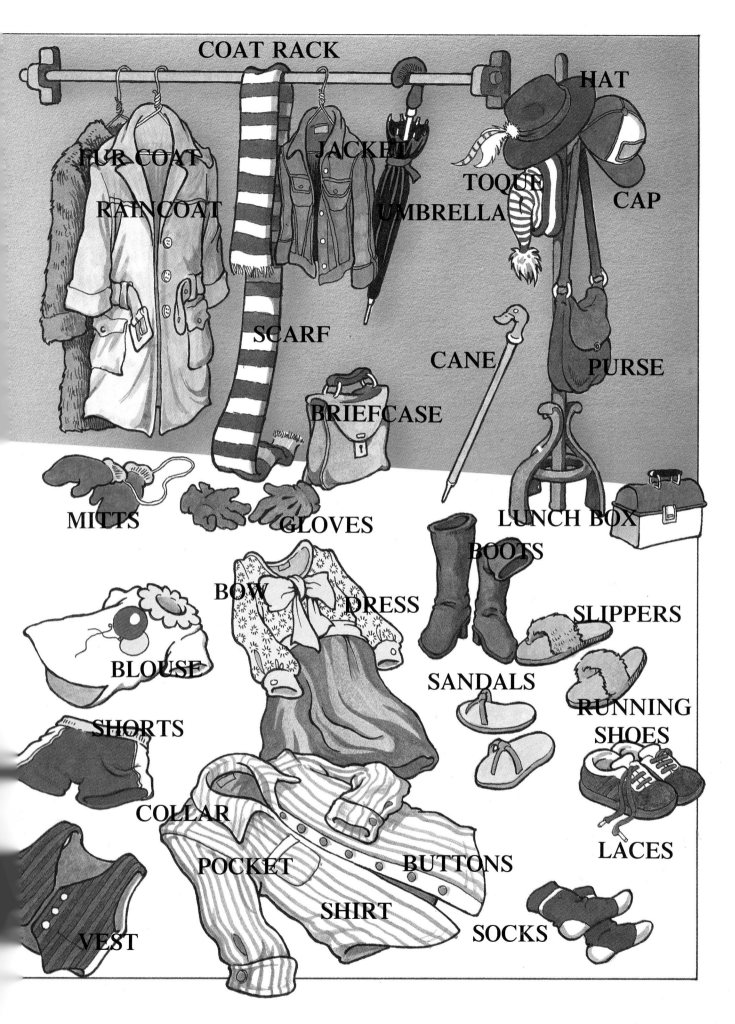

COAT RACK

HAT

FUR COAT

JACKET

TOQUE

CAP

RAINCOAT

UMBRELLA

SCARF

CANE

PURSE

BRIEFCASE

MITTS

GLOVES

LUNCH BOX

BOOTS

BOW

DRESS

SLIPPERS

BLOUSE

SANDALS

RUNNING
SHOES

SHORTS

COLLAR

LACES

POCKET

BUTTONS

SHIRT

SOCKS

VEST

IN THE KITCHEN

CLOCK

REFRIGERATOR

WALL SOCKET

FLOOR WAX

TOASTER

BOY
SON
BROTHER

GIRL
DAUGHTER
SISTER

BROOM

GARBAGE CAN

MOP

BUCKET

STAIRS

CEREAL

IRONING BOARD

SPOON

TABLE

IRON

BABY

GLASS

BUTTER

BOWL

KETCHUP

TOAST

PEPPER

SALT

SUGAR

WINDOW

CUPBOARD

MAN
FATHER
HUSBAND

OVEN MITTS

DISHES

TAP

POT

TOWEL

COOKIE JAR

WOMAN
MOTHER
WIFE

STOOL

BLENDER

DRAWERS

KETTLE

PLUG

STOVE

DOG DISH

TEAPOT

COUNTER

KNIFE

CHAIR

OVEN

PLATE

FORK

FLOOR

MUG

ON THE BUS

SOLDIER

HANDRAIL

ASTRONAUTS

CHEF

CLOWN

DANCER

FISHERMAN

AXE

LUMBERJACK

NET

FARMER

FIREMAN

POLICEWOMAN

BUS DRIVER

OVERALLS

HELMET

BOOTS

LUNCH BOX

MINER

IN THE TOWN

STREET SIGNS

WINDOW WASHER

HOSPITAL

WALK

CINEMA

SIREN

AMBULANCE

SUBWAY

ROAD

PARKING METER

16

CRANE

SKYSCRAPER

ENCON

FLAG

LAMPPOST

ZET'S

FIRE STATION

BANK

FIRE TRUCK

BUS

POLICE

IDEWALK

CROSSWALK

CURB

POLICE CAR

ON THE STREET

BILLBOARD

CAMERA SHOP

WAITER

TERRAC

BARREL

HARDWARE STORE

BUTCHER SHOP

RESTAURAN

AT THE SHOPPING MALL

BOUTIQUE

CUSTOMER

SALESPERSON

DISPLAY

ASHCA

ALLEY

BOOK STORE

SIGN

MUNCHIES

DELIVERY VAN

PLANTER

BAKERY

ICE CREAM PARLOR

RECORD STORE

DRUG STORE

SHOE STORE

POSTER

BENCH

SHOPPING BAG

PIES

TRAY

BREAD

FISHMONGER

CHICKEN

FISH

BAKER

STEAK

PEPPERS

FREEZER

LETTUCE

SAUSAGES

CORN

BEANS

POTATOES

SACK

STRAWBERRIES

BLUEBERRIES

CHERRIES

RASPBERRIES

ONIONS

UMBRELLA

BANANAS

BOTTLES

CHEESE

COFFEE

EGGS

BUTTER

MILK

PINEAPPLE

SCALE

MUSHROOMS

CASH REGISTER

TOMATOES

CRATES

APPLES

PEARS

GRAPES

BARREL

ORANGES

LEMONS

PEACHES

THE DOCTOR

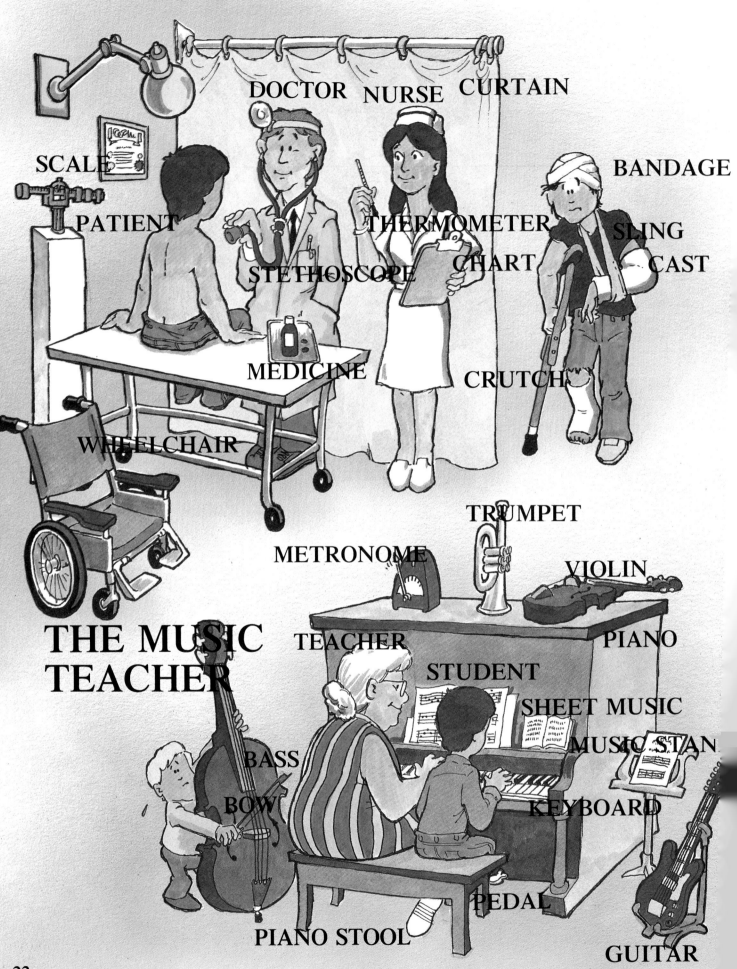

DOCTOR NURSE CURTAIN

SCALE

BANDAGE

PATIENT

THERMOMETER

SLING

STETHOSCOPE CHART CAST

MEDICINE

CRUTCH

WHEELCHAIR

TRUMPET

METRONOME

VIOLIN

THE MUSIC TEACHER

TEACHER

PIANO

STUDENT

SHEET MUSIC

MUSIC STAND

BASS

BOW

KEYBOARD

PEDAL

PIANO STOOL

GUITAR

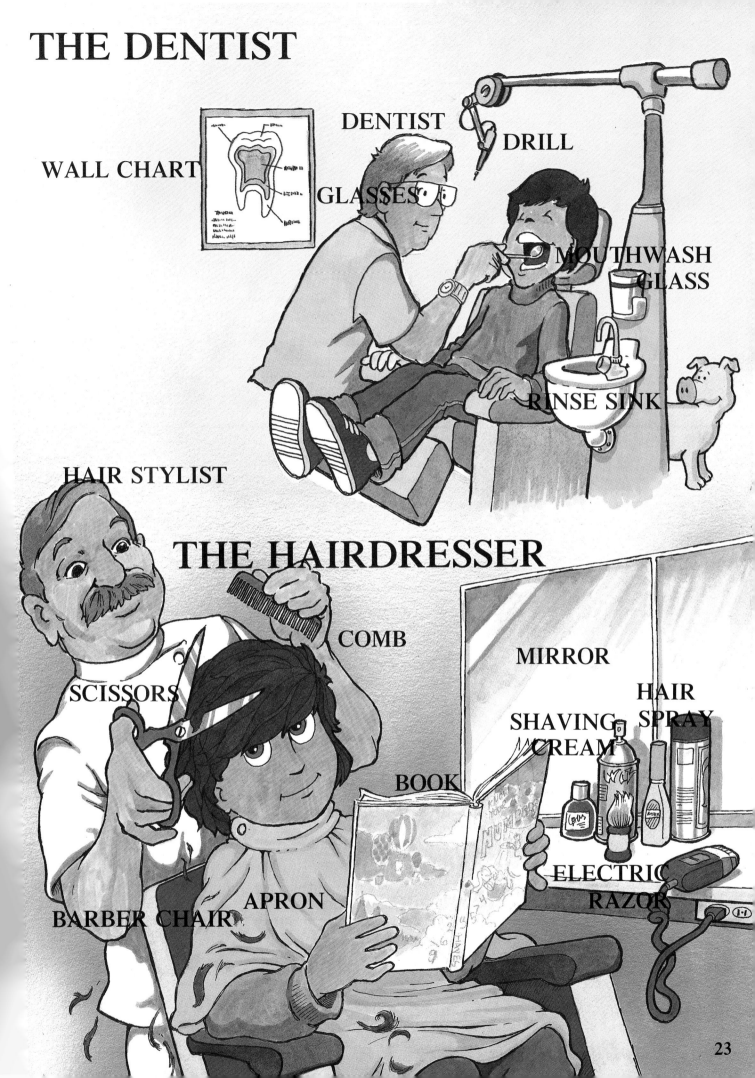

THE DENTIST

WALL CHART

DENTIST

DRILL

GLASSES

MOUTHWASH GLASS

RINSE SINK

HAIR STYLIST

THE HAIRDRESSER

COMB

MIRROR

SCISSORS

HAIR SPRAY

SHAVING CREAM

BOOK

ELECTRIC RAZOR

BARBER CHAIR

APRON

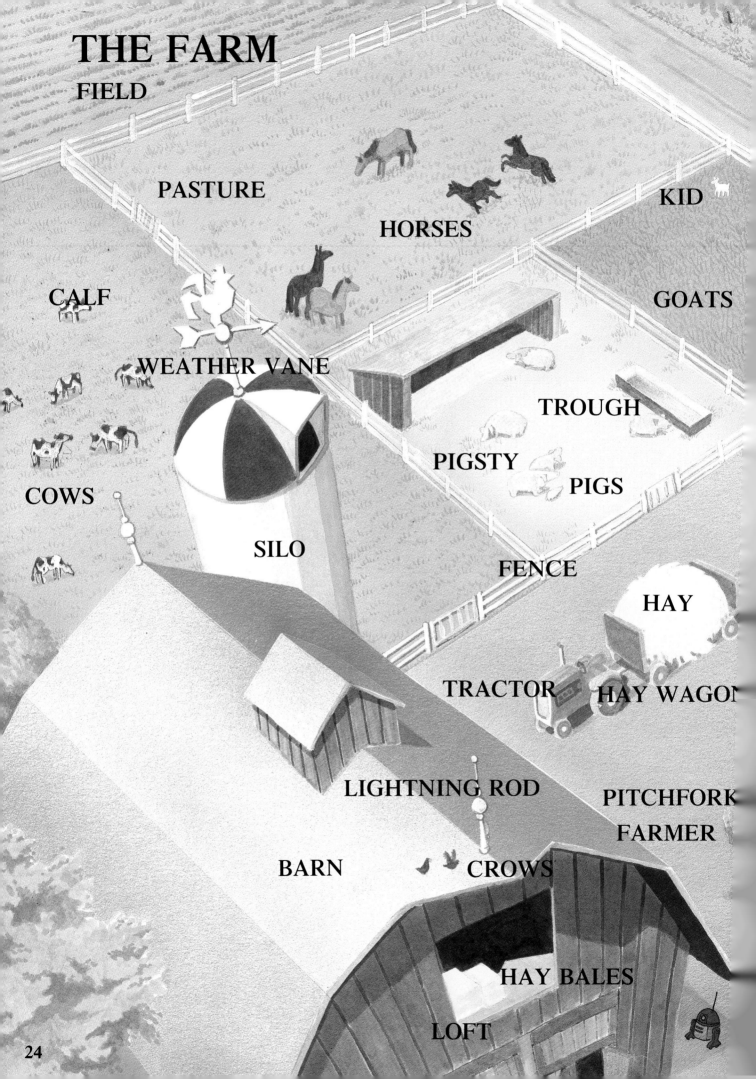

THE FARM

FIELD

PASTURE

HORSES

KID

CALF

GOATS

WEATHER VANE

TROUGH

PIGSTY

PIGS

COWS

SILO

FENCE

HAY

TRACTOR

HAY WAGON

LIGHTNING ROD

PITCHFORK

FARMER

BARN

CROWS

HAY BALES

LOFT

24

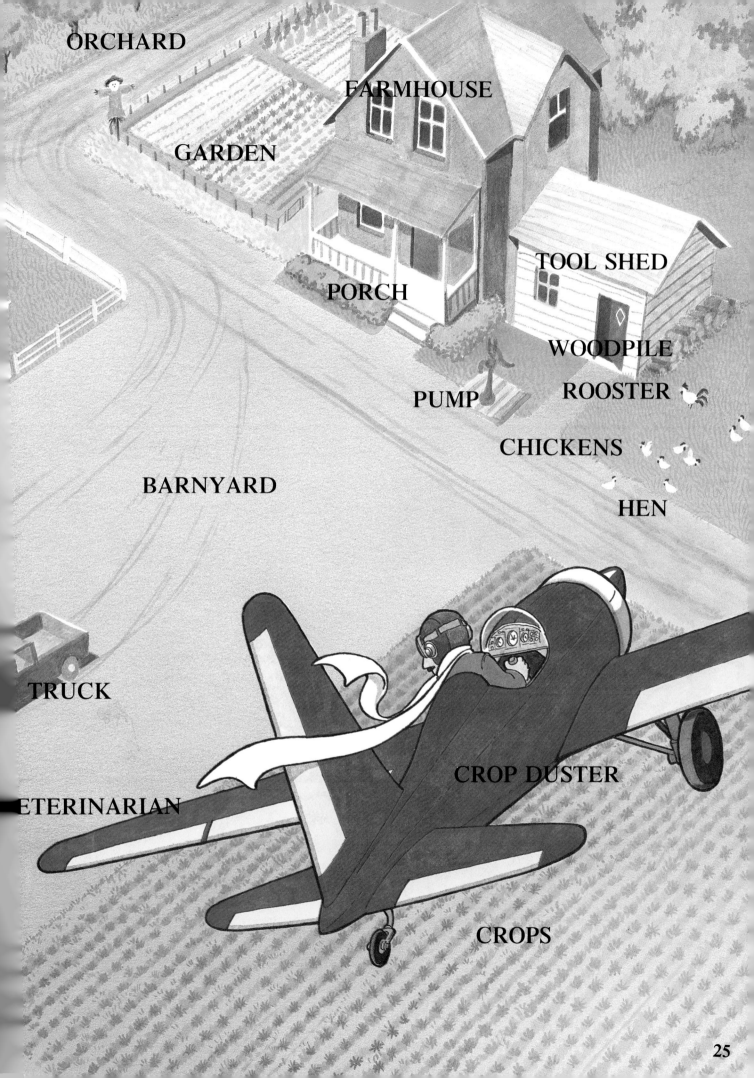

ORCHARD

FARMHOUSE

GARDEN

TOOL SHED

PORCH

WOODPILE

PUMP

ROOSTER

CHICKENS

BARNYARD

HEN

TRUCK

CROP DUSTER

ETERINARIAN

CROPS

SPRING

RAINBOW

STAG

DOE

FAWN

RABBITS

WORM

EARTH

ROBIN

GEESE

BABY BIRDS

BUDS

NEST

RAIN

FARMER

TRACTOR

DISC

GROUNDHOGS

DISC HARROW

BURROW

GRASS

FURROWS

SKUNKS

FIELD MICE

27

SUMMER

PARACHUTE

PARACHUTIST

PINE TREES

CAMPER

WOODS

BEACH

PICNIC TABLE

LOGS

TENTS

SCUBA DIVING

BONFIRE

SINGING

BEACH BALL

SUNBATHE

CRAB

SAND

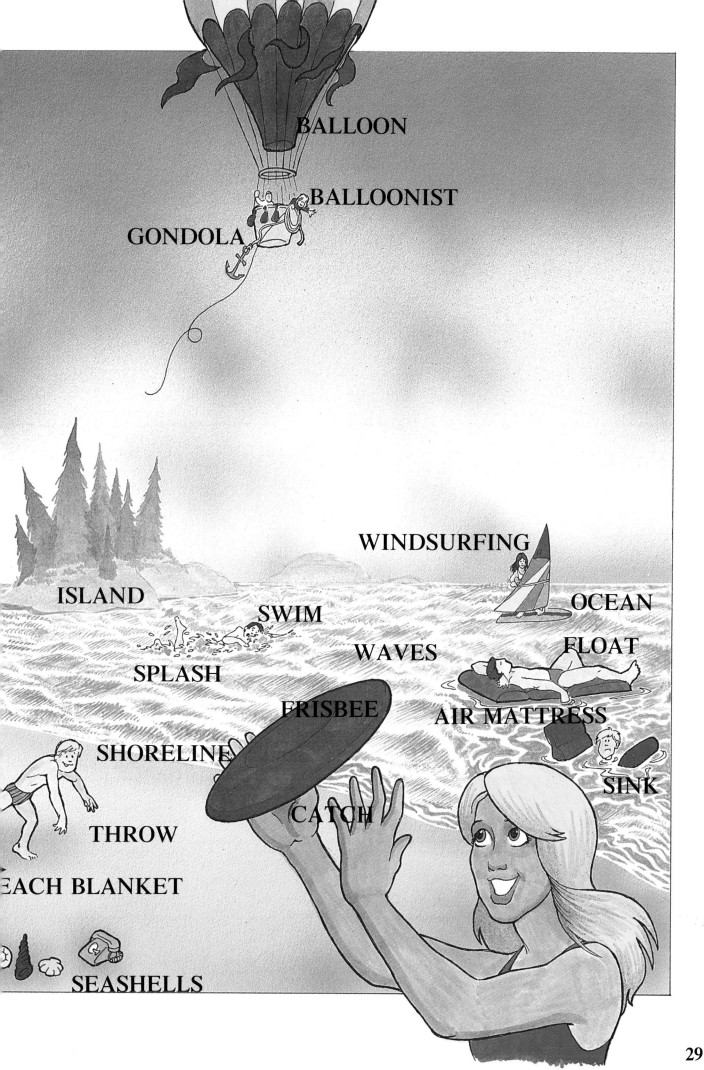

BALLOON

BALLOONIST

GONDOLA

WINDSURFING

ISLAND

OCEAN

SWIM

WAVES

FLOAT

SPLASH

FRISBEE

AIR MATTRESS

SHORELINE

SINK

CATCH

THROW

EACH BLANKET

SEASHELLS

FALL

LEAVES

SHOUT

TREE HOUSE

CLING

BELL

TREE

SNAP

PLATFORM

WAVE

FALL

BROWN

PINK

ROPE LADDER

CARRY

TRIP

TRUNK

STAND

30

REACH

BRANCH

ORANGE

BALANCE

BLACK

STEPS

HOLD

SIT

VIOLET

BLUE

CLIMB

RED

ROPE

PURPLE

GREEN

WHITE

YELLOW

JUMP

HANG

GRAY

SWING

CRAWL

GROUND

31

WINTER

SNOWMAN

SKIING

SKI POLES

IGLOO

SKIS

EARMUFFS

SNOW

SNOWBALL FIGHT

PARKA

SLED

LAUGH

PUSH

ST. BERNARD

SNOWMOBILE

BENCH

SKATES

HOCKEY STICK

SNOWSHOES

PEAK

MOUNTAIN

CHRISTMAS LIGHTS

ICICLES

SKI MASK

LODGE

SHIVER

SNOWDRIFTS

HUSKY

COLD

SNOW SUIT

ICE

PUCK

TRAINS

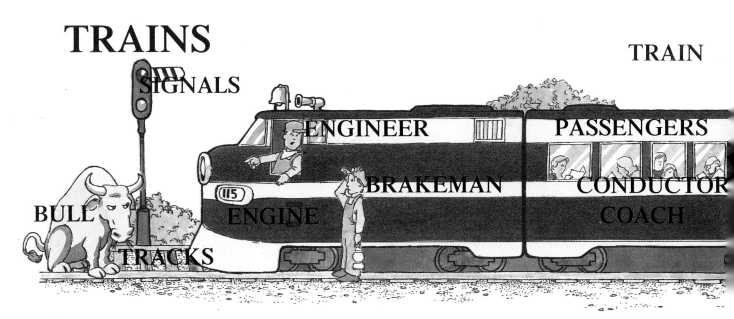

TRAIN

SIGNALS

ENGINEER

PASSENGERS

BRAKEMAN

CONDUCTOR

BULL

ENGINE

COACH

TRACKS

BOATS

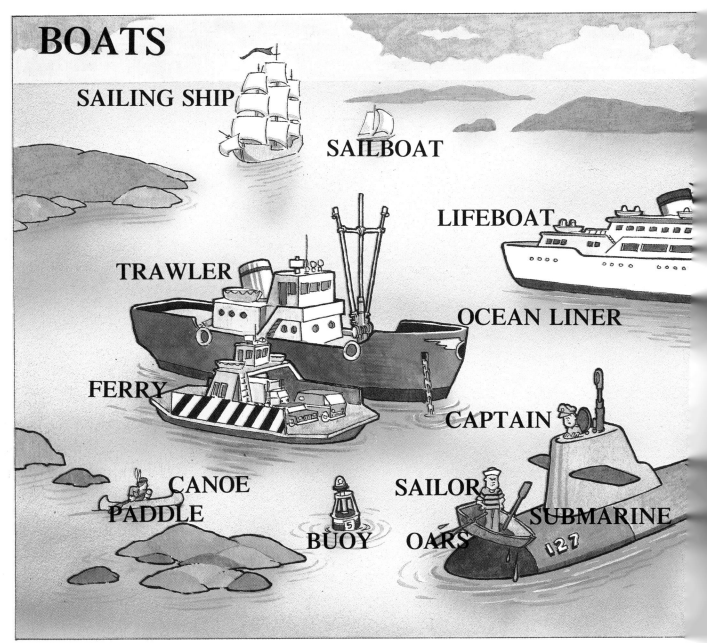

SAILING SHIP

SAILBOAT

LIFEBOAT

TRAWLER

OCEAN LINER

FERRY

CAPTAIN

CANOE

SAILOR

PADDLE

SUBMARINE

BUOY

OARS

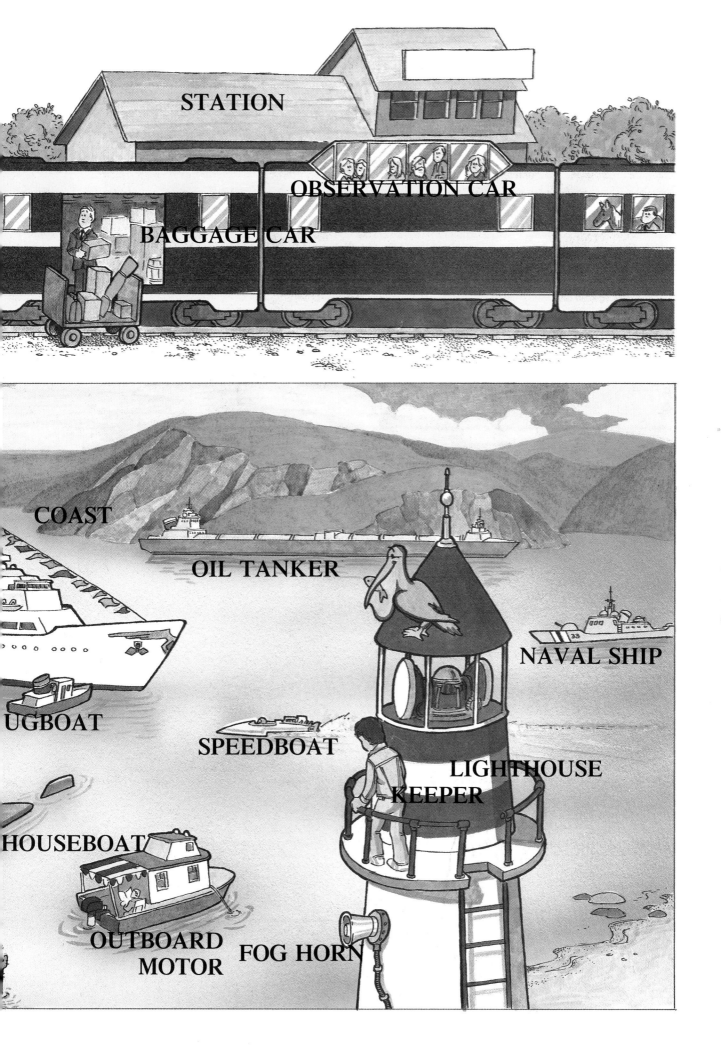

STATION

OBSERVATION CAR

BAGGAGE CAR

COAST

OIL TANKER

UGBOAT

SPEEDBOAT

NAVAL SHIP

LIGHTHOUSE
KEEPER

HOUSEBOAT

OUTBOARD
MOTOR

FOG HORN

PLANES

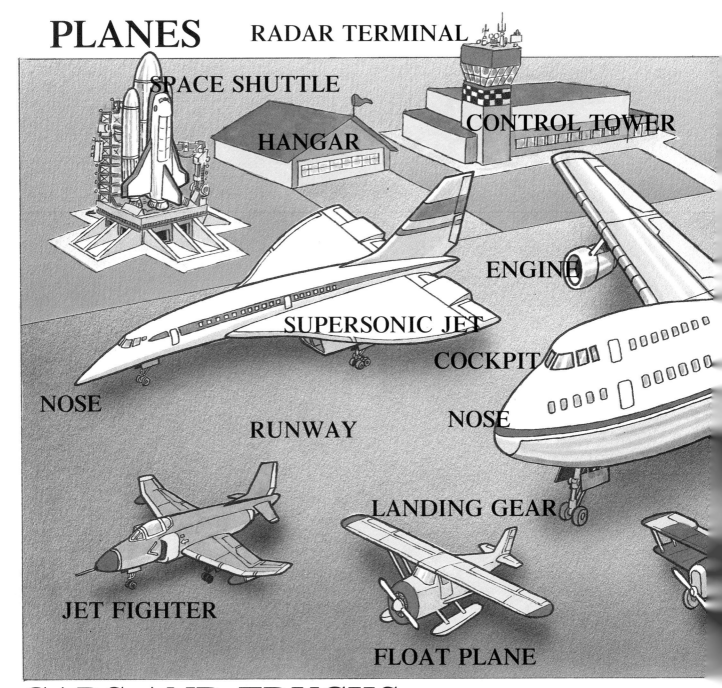

RADAR TERMINAL

SPACE SHUTTLE

CONTROL TOWER

HANGAR

ENGINE

SUPERSONIC JET

COCKPIT

NOSE

NOSE

RUNWAY

LANDING GEAR

JET FIGHTER

FLOAT PLANE

CARS AND TRUCKS

FOG LAMPS

TARPAULIN

REAR VIEW MIRROR

COMPACT CAR

LICENSE PLATE

RACING CAR

BUMPER

PICKUP

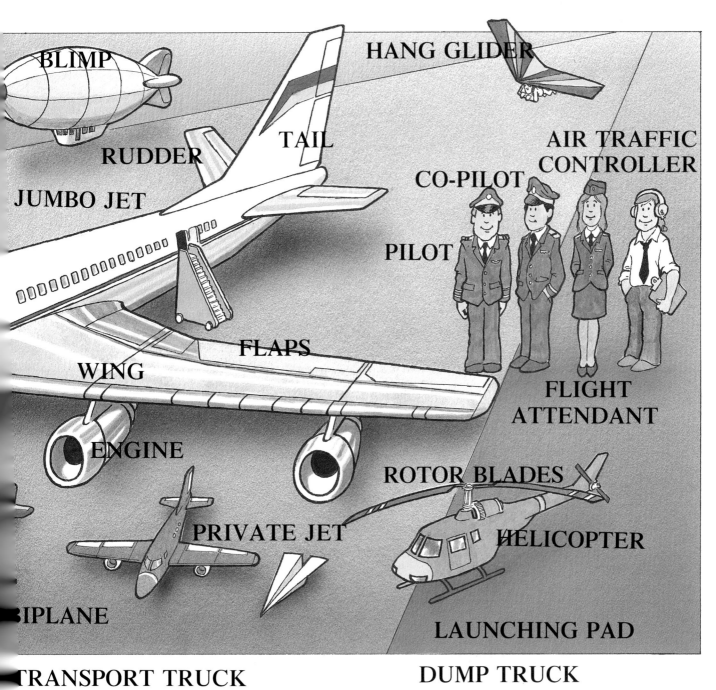

BLIMP

HANG GLIDER

RUDDER

TAIL

JUMBO JET

AIR TRAFFIC CONTROLLER

CO-PILOT

PILOT

FLAPS

WING

FLIGHT ATTENDANT

ENGINE

ROTOR BLADES

PRIVATE JET

HELICOPTER

BIPLANE

LAUNCHING PAD

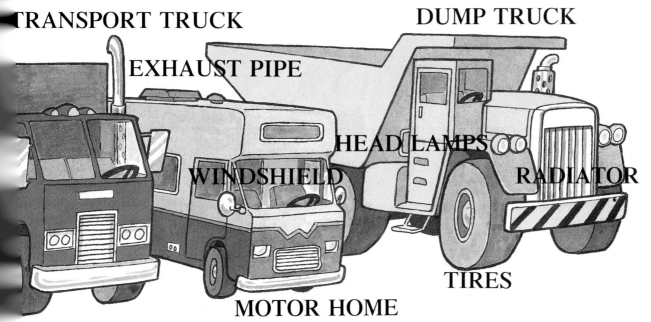

TRANSPORT TRUCK

DUMP TRUCK

EXHAUST PIPE

HEAD LAMPS

WINDSHIELD

RADIATOR

TIRES

MOTOR HOME

SCHOOL DAYS

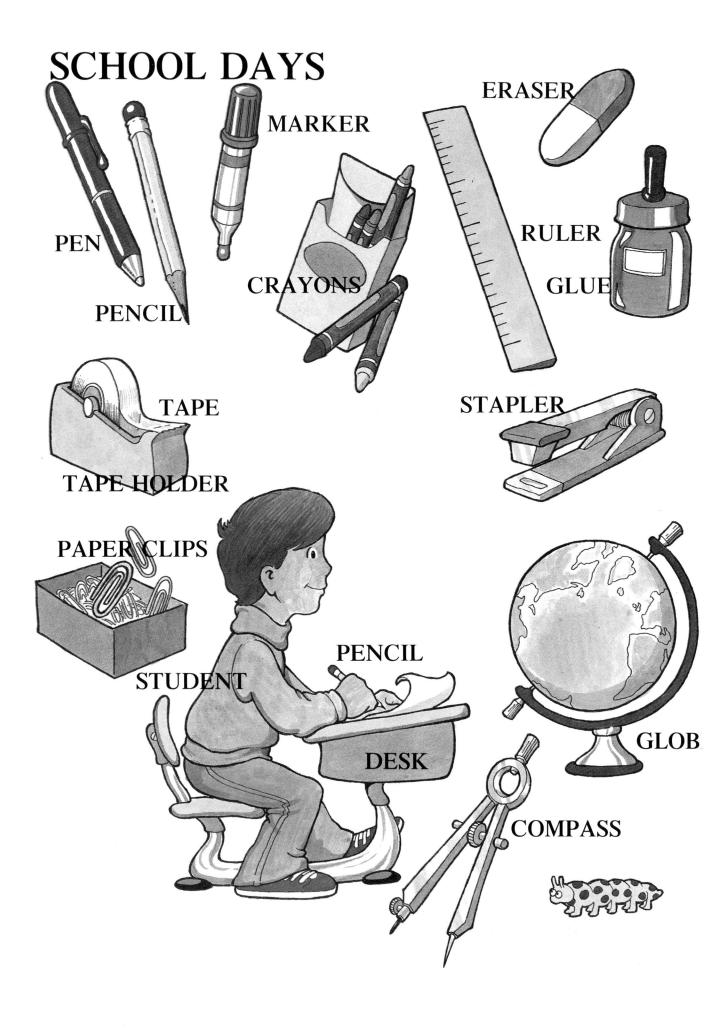

PEN

PENCIL

MARKER

ERASER

RULER

GLUE

CRAYONS

TAPE

TAPE HOLDER

STAPLER

PAPER CLIPS

STUDENT

PENCIL

DESK

GLOB

COMPASS

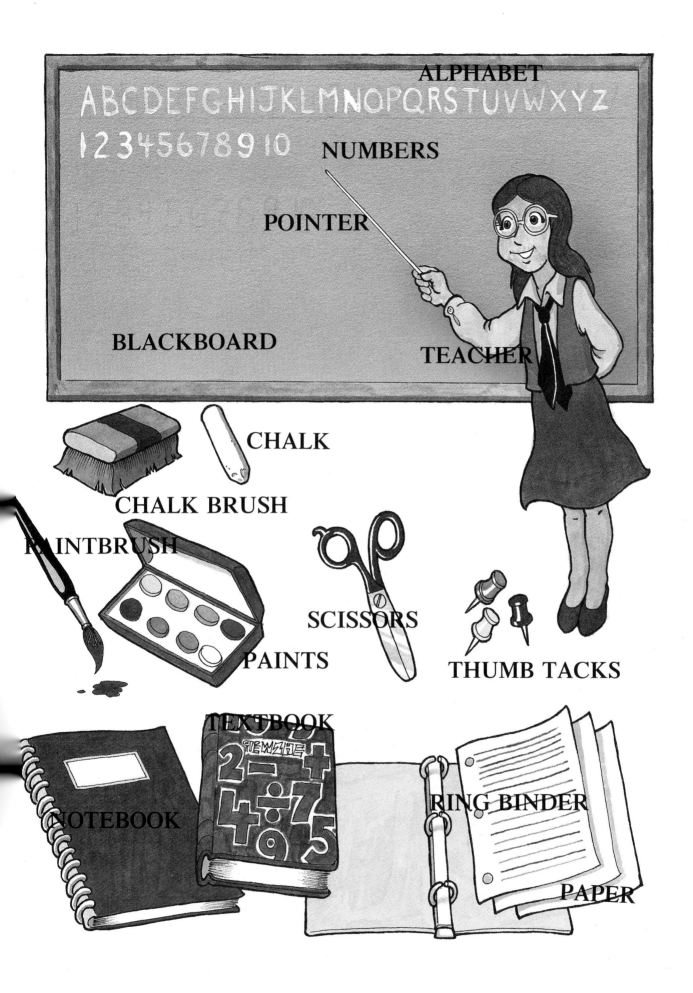

ALPHABET

NUMBERS

POINTER

BLACKBOARD

TEACHER

CHALK

CHALK BRUSH

PAINTBRUSH

SCISSORS

PAINTS

THUMB TACKS

TEXTBOOK

RING BINDER

NOTEBOOK

PAPER

PARTY TIME

STREAMERS

DRAGON COSTUME

HELMET

SWORD

CROWN

SHIELD

KING

QUEEN

PARROT

DEVIL

WITCH

PIRATE

BALLOONS

VIKING MONSTER

FEATHERS

MASK

TAIL

AXE

INDIAN

WAND BEARD

HALO HAT

ANGEL WIZARD

WINGS COWBOY

GHOST HOLSTER

VAMPIRE

PUNCH

41

SOUND SIGHT AND MOTION

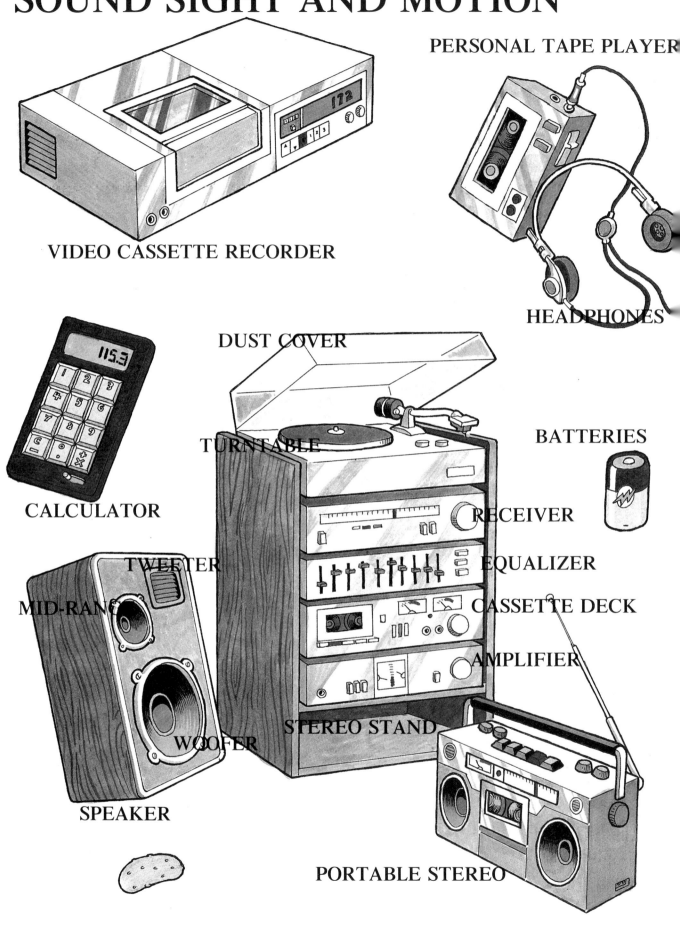

PERSONAL TAPE PLAYER

VIDEO CASSETTE RECORDER

HEADPHONES

DUST COVER

BATTERIES

CALCULATOR

TURNTABLE

TWEETER

RECEIVER

MID-RANGE

EQUALIZER

CASSETTE DECK

AMPLIFIER

STEREO STAND

WOOFER

SPEAKER

PORTABLE STEREO

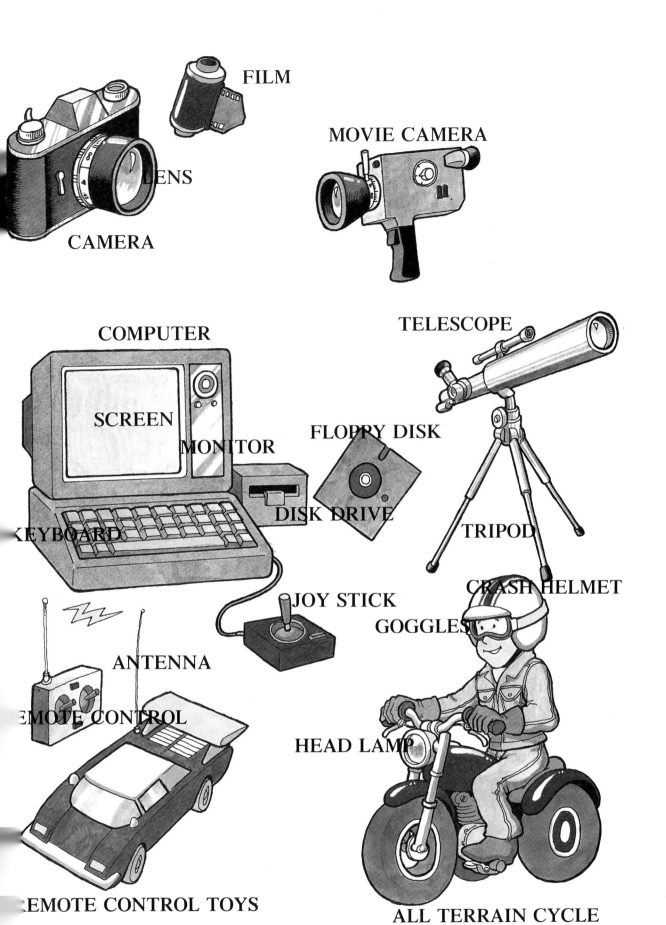

FILM

MOVIE CAMERA

LENS

CAMERA

COMPUTER

TELESCOPE

SCREEN

MONITOR

FLOPPY DISK

KEYBOARD

DISK DRIVE

TRIPOD

JOY STICK

CRASH HELMET

GOGGLES

ANTENNA

REMOTE CONTROL

HEAD LAMP

REMOTE CONTROL TOYS

ALL TERRAIN CYCLE

ANIMALS

BEAR

RHINOCEROS

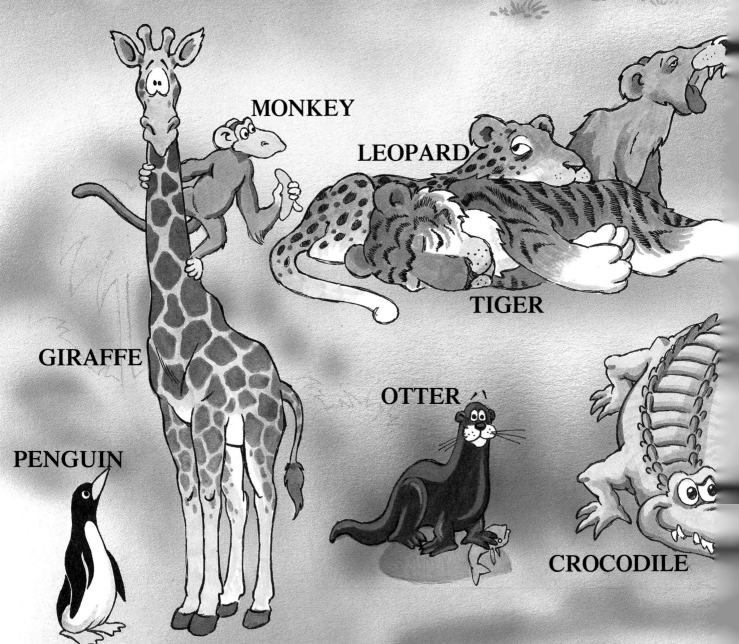

MONKEY

LEOPARD

TIGER

GIRAFFE

OTTER

PENGUIN

CROCODILE

ELEPHANT

SNAKE

MOUSE

MOOSE

WILD PIG

IN THE GARDEN

BEE

INCHWORM

SPIDER WEB

MOT[H]

SPIDER PLANTS

SPIDER

WINE

IVY

HUMMING BIRD

BUTTERFLY

SUNFLOWER

PETALS

ROSES

LEAF

STEM

TULI[P]

WATERING CAN

LADY BUG

FLOWER POTS

SEEDS

DANDELION

BULBS

GRASSHOPPER

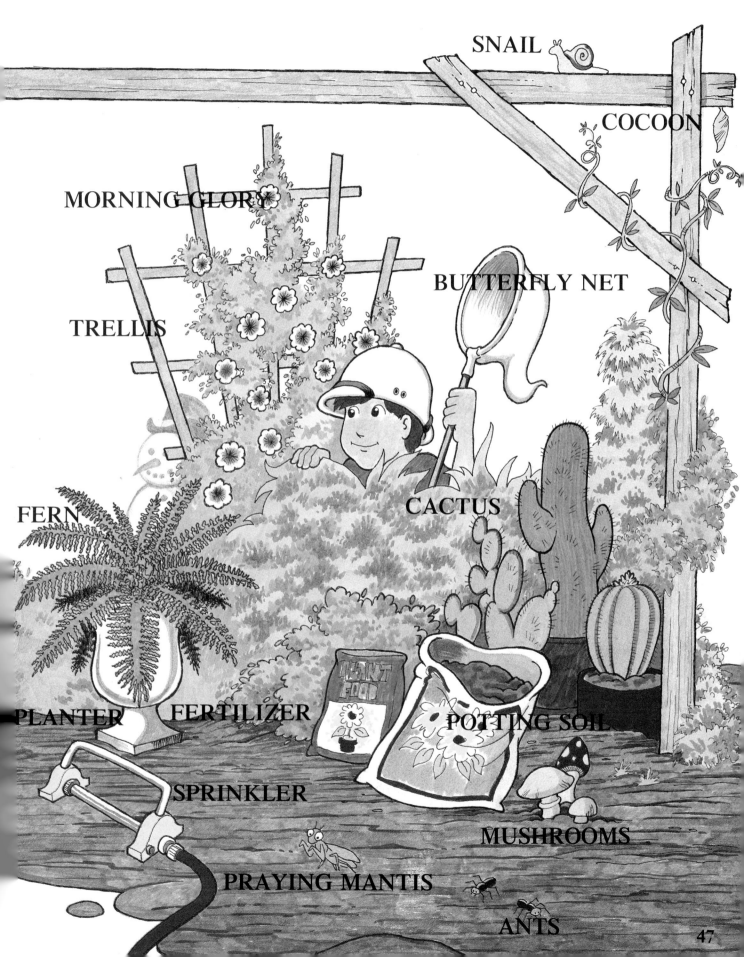

FLY

SNAIL

COCOON

MORNING GLORY

BUTTERFLY NET

TRELLIS

FERN

CACTUS

PLANTER

FERTILIZER

POTTING SOIL

SPRINKLER

MUSHROOMS

PRAYING MANTIS

ANTS